I0410009

WHAT THE WORLD SHOULD KNOW ABOUT…

BLACK HISTORY IN THE USA

Walter G. Luttrell

© 2013 Walter G. Luttrell
All rights reserved
Blog: www.learnaboutblackhistory.blogspot.com

Published by eBookIt.com
ISBN-13: 978-1-4566-1906-0

No part of this book may be reproduced in any form or by any electronic or mechanical means including information storage and retrieval systems, without permission in writing from the author. The only exception is by a reviewer, who may quote short excerpts in a review.

Let's start with this question: How might the U.S. be different today (2012) IF the millions of Black slaves freed after the Civil War had been given the (briefly) promised "40 acres and a mule," to get a "start" in life...AND the same access to educational and economic opportunities as Whites, thereafter?

Think about it! Would there be Black slums/ghettos in virtually every U.S. city? Would the percentage of Black citizens receiving "public aid" (welfare) be the same? With equal access to educational and economic opportunity for the past (?) 150 years, would there be more Black leaders in corporate, educational, and institutional America? And, with such equal opportunity, would the U.S. prison populations be different, smaller? How would life FEEL in the USA, with less racial tension, anger, and hostility?

Please... just stop and try to "visualize" for a moment what the United States of America MIGHT be like today if Blacks... oh, and other minorities, and women... ALL Americans... for the past century and a half had been treated equally? Then read this little "booklet" and go to our web blog, www.learnaboutblackhistory.blogspot.com, and share your thoughts. This booklet focuses on the Black experience in America, but the pain of discrimination has probably been felt, in some way, by ALL of us: especially, women, other minorities, the disabled, the "different!" Go ahead; read, think, and respond. Don't be afraid; the result could be very healthy, healing... even hopeful! There is much important work to be done for the United States of America to reach its full potential, and this exercise may help clear our minds for the challenges ahead.

AUTHOR'S NOTE: After the infamous U.S. "race riots" of the 1960's there was much debate about the importance of "including" the history of African-Americans more fully in U.S. history text books. From exploration of "the new world" as <u>free</u> mariners, through the degradation of slavery and segregation (following "emancipation"), Blacks made extraordinary contributions to the achievements that made this country great. Today, though our President is Black, Studies show Americans, of ALL races, remain woefully under-informed of those contributions… and many heroic Whites and others who supported Black civil rights… at great peril to their own lives. This little "booklet" is intended only as an "educational supplement." It is released electronically, as an eBook, now and (hopefully later) in printed form also so people anywhere in the world can, in a very short time, gain a better understanding of the Black experience in America. *Please read then recommend this publication to everyone you know.* For many, *THIS is a "starting point" - for learning about the history of Black people in the evolution of the United States of America!*

CONTENTS

FOREWORD

"You Been Set Free" "When freedom came, my mama said Old Master called all of 'em to his house, and he said, 'you all free, we ain't got nothing to do with you no more. Go on away. We don't whop you no more, go on your way.'

My mama said they go on off, then they come back and stand around, just looking at him and Old Mistress. They give 'em something to eat and he say, 'Go on away, you don't belong to us no more. You been freed.' They go away and they kept coming back. They didn't have no place to go and nothing to eat. From what she said, they had a terrible time. She said it was bad times. Some took sick and had no 'tention and died. Seemed like it was four or five years before they got to places they could live.

They all got scattered . . Old Master every time they go back say, You all go on away. You been set free. You have to look out for yourselves now.'

—An ex-slave's account in Lay My Burden Down:
A Folk History of Slavery, Ben Botkin, 1945

The above statement reveals the plight of a people facing a freedom almost as formidable as the bondage from which they were released. The vindictive attitude of many Southern slave holders was exemplified by the cry, "The Yankees freed you, now let the Yankees feed you." Freedom without food, shelter, clothing or the means to get them was to the black man — like the one above — an obvious step backwards. Despairing of a place to settle, rootless bands of "freedmen" roamed the South in that vague and hazy world between waking and sleeping, life and death, bondage and freedom. "The South was a shambles, its major cities gutted or shelled, its farms neglected, crops ungathered, banks closed, Confederate money worthless, and about 1/3 of its male citizens killed or wounded," according to Langston Hughes in a "Pictorial History of the Negro in America." Both black and white people of the South faced the immense task of re-establishing their lives. But the immediate future of freed slaves was indeed dark. To alleviate the situation, Congress established the Freedmen's Bureau, in March 1865, to be administered by the Army and headed by Major General Oliver O. Howard.

Against violent southern opposition the Freedmen's Bureau, supported by Federal troops, distributed rations and medicine to the poor, black and white alike. The Bureau built or helped to build more than 4,000 schools staffed with 9,000 teachers who served almost 250,000 black students. At the time of the Emancipation, only one in every ten of the newly freed could read and write. Thousands of northern whites went to the South to teach at the Bureau's request, despite hostile threats. The task of teaching, especially under such conditions, seemed impossible. But, when the Bureau was abolished in 1870, approximately 21 per cent of the newly freed were literate.

History books have tended to obscure rather than credit those people, black and white, who took up the burden of educating Blacks for diffusion into American culture before and after the Civil war. Their contributions to OUR society have been seldom published. For this reason, this booklet is dedicated to those who suffered, sacrificed and, sometimes, gave their lives that this country might some day take a lesson from history and produce an example for future societies in the interests of all people.

We cannot, of course, begin to cover all of those who were instrumental in the spiritual and educational emancipation of the oppressed. Thus we have tried to construct an interesting and concise supplement which we hope will render stimulating insight into "the Black experience in America."

SOME TAUGHT...

"THE THINKER"
by Rodin

If you can keep your head when all about you
    Are losing theirs and blaming it on you,
If you can trust yourself when all men doubt you
    But make allowance for their doubting too,
If you can wait and not be tired by waiting,
    Or being lied about, don't deal in lies,
Or being hated, don't give way to hating,
    And yet don't look too good, nor talk too wise.

There have been many educated people of color in America since the birth of William Tucker in 1624, recognized as the first black child born in America. Education is a means by which men rise above their given positions and reach that ". . . equal station to which the Laws of Nature and of Nature's God entitle them. . . ."

Although it was generally against the law to expose slaves to book-learning - because knowledge was suspected of spawning notions of freedom - some insisted on learning. More important, possibly, were those whites who initially trusted their own beliefs and were determined to spread knowledge wherever it would be received.

An exemplary case was that of English actress, Fanny Kemble, who came to America and married a Georgia plantation owner. She wrote of a sixteen-year-old slave boy who had asked her to teach him to read, "I will do it . . . and yet it is simply breaking (the) laws of the government under which I am serving." Then she declared, "Unrighteous laws are made to be broken ... I'll teach every other creature that wants to learn." There were others who recognized the need for black literacy and through them America was given the minds and services of many persons, whose echoing voices are still heard today. Some of these are presented here in brief profile.

****John B. Russwurm** (1799-1851) was the first black college graduate in America, receiving his degree from Bowdoin College in Maine, 1826. Russwurm was an ardent supporter of abolitionism and believed that blacks should organize in their quest for freedom. Hoping to spread his beliefs and support emancipation efforts, Russwurm later co-edited the Journal of Freedom in March of 1827, which was the first Black newspaper in the U.S. Following those achievements, and prompted by his interest in Black colonization, Mr. Russwurm went abroad to become the first Superintendent of Schools in Liberia.

****The Jubilee Singers** were organized to raise money when it looked as if the Fisk School, established in 1866 by the American Missionary Association, would have to close its doors for lack of money. Nine young men and women, shoddily dressed but determined to prevail, began a tour of the north to sing spirituals in a fund-raising campaign. Their singing improved with time, and when their performances began to draw tears, they were on the road to success. Who would have imagined the tour to last seven years with a visit to the White House preceding a trip around Europe? They returned with $150,000 to help the little school which is now Fisk University in Nashville, Tennessee.

****Booker T. Washington** (1856-1915) was born a slave in West Virginia. He worked in the salt mines of Virginia until he heard about a school called Hampton Institute where black children learned trades. He resolved to attend Hampton some day and began preparation by learning his ABC's after work. At fifteen he was ready and began his journey to Hampton by stagecoach, but ended it walking because his money ran out.

Working his way through school as a house painter, Washington was greatly impressed with the dedication of Hampton's founder, General Samuel C. Armstrong, and the school's New England teachers. Of them he wrote, "What a rare set of human beings," declaring that their role in the post-Civil War education of Blacks would "make one of the most thrilling parts in the history of this country." Deciding that teaching was a worthy cause, Washington's itinerary carried him home again where he taught black children by day, grown-ups by night.

He later returned to teach at Hampton where he answered a call from a white banker and a black mechanic in Alabama to open a school there for rural Blacks. When the school opened, Washington was the only teacher. Between classes in an old church, he and his students constructed a new building in 1881, marking the birth of Tuskegee Institute — the pioneer example of an independent industrial school.

******Mary McLeod Bethune** (1875-1955) labored in cotton fields as a child and walked five miles daily to a mission school. She later decided to pass her knowledge down to others and opened her own school in Florida with orange crates for benches. The school, which was to become Bethune-Cookman College, grew as did the prestige of its founder. She became a friend of the Roosevelts and a powerful figure in New Deal policies relating to Blacks. Even if taken out of context, this quote from the lady educator is certainly applicable today. "There is now before us an unparalleled opportunity, this is our day! Doors will open everywhere. The flood tide of a new life is coming in."

John Chavis
Helped shatter myth of "Negro" inferiority

****John Chavis, before the turn of the 18th century, became the educational product of a wager between two prominent gentlemen of North Carolina. Chavis' supporter sent him to Princeton for a time. Chavis returned, in 1805, to shatter the myth, locally, of Black inferiority and to "teach" the sons of other prominent gentlemen. Chavis spent his evenings enlightening the Black children of the area.

George Washington Carver
Turned down a fortune to teach his "own people"

******George Washington Carver** (1864-1943) was a phenomenon of selflessness. While living on Moses Carver's plantation in Missouri, shortly after the Civil War, George and his mother were abducted by night-riding slave snatchers who ignored the Emancipation Proclamation and sold Blacks in territories south and west of Missouri. Moses Carver, however, was one of those rare and warm persons who often are instrumental in cultivating great men. He sent one of his men after the raiders with money to buy the mother and infant back.

But the mother had been sold and the raiders would part with the baby for no less than the cash plus the valuable racing horse which Carver's agent rode. It was done. George Washington Carver returned to Moses Carver who, along with his wife, raised George and his older brother, who had evaded the raiders, as their own.

The boys were encouraged to read and when curiosity seized young George he was already hotly pursuing education. He received permission to attend a school for Blacks at the age of ten and after absorbing what the school offered, traveled to Fort Scott, Kansas, to complete high school. Working his way through college as a launderer and cook, young Carver was encouraged to study music and art, for which he had a natural gift. His real interest, however, was in plants; why they grow, what gives them color and the beauty of nature's pattern of "living things."

George studied for personal pleasure and seemed to shun all rewards for his work. In his life-long work at Tuskegee Institute, where Carver spent forty years in teaching and research, he turned his attention to the development of the "simple things" about him. For instance, he developed nearly three hundred by-products of the peanut including cheese, breakfast foods, soap, and even nitroglycerin.

Carver refused an offer to work with Thomas Edison in his New Jersey laboratory for $175,000 yearly because he preferred to stay with his own people who he felt needed him in their struggle for economic independence. For the same reason, he later turned down a rich offer from Russia. George W. Carver —a truly magnanimous individual!

MANY WERE KILLED...

CRISPUS ATTUCKS
First martyr/American Revolutionary War

If you can dream--and not make dreams your master,
    If you can think--and not make thoughts your aim;
If you can meet with Triumph and Disaster
    And treat those two impostors just the same;
If you can bear to hear the truth you've spoken
    Twisted by knaves to make a trap for fools,
Or watch the things you gave your life to, broken,
    And stoop and build 'em up with worn-out tools:

In the course of history there have been an almost infinite number of people killed, murdered, slaughtered; whichever term is used makes little difference . . . they are gone. Among these countless obituaries we find a few, maybe less considering the whole, who gave their lives for the principles in which they believed. These were the people whose dreams were ended suddenly, often violently, with the insensibility of blind, ignorant rage. The martyr has often met with disaster but their triumph or anonymity belongs to history and the course it takes. Indeed their words may later be twisted even as their body was in dying — and for the dead the stooping is ended. But the "things" they gave their lives to may never be broken. Around the world, those who know U.S. history may remember MLK, JFK, RFK, Malcolm, Medgar, et. al... hopefully this little booklet gives them much MORE to think about and explore.

******Crispus Attucks** (1723-1770) is generally recognized as the first martyr of the American Revolution. Attucks was killed in the Boston Massacre, March 5, 1770, twenty years after he escaped from slavery to become a merchant seaman. Attucks, like most of the colonists, was angry about the Navigation Acts imposed by the British.

A number of fights broke out between British soldiers and civilians and, in a confrontation on the Boston Commons, Crispus Attucks along with five other patriots, was shot to death supporting the cause of American liberty.

******The Reverend George Lee** — There comes a time in the lives of some when a decision is made; or maybe it is always there and finally accepted. And so it was decided that children shouldn't starve in the "land of plenty;" that it isn't acceptable that some must cower in the "home of the brave"; that human beings shouldn't be kindling for the "melting pot," and that there is no room for human bondage in the "land of the free."

Reverend George Lee longed for the day when Black men could stand up and be counted, but he was no longer willing to stand idly by in the waiting.

George Lee had come a long way since he was born in Edwards, Mississippi in 1904. After graduating from a "plantation" high school, Lee took a correspondence course in typesetting while working on the New Orleans banana docks. During those years, Lee led a rather typical Black Southern life, all the while resisting an urge to join the ministry. But his inner self longed for release and he finally yielded to his real calling.

Lee became a pastor, but one of a new breed. It was said that, "From the beginning he felt a lingering discontent with pastoring in the fashion of most Black preachers of the day . . for Lee it was not enough to orate about heaven and eat free chicken dinners on Sunday." Reverend Lee well remembered the plight of Black people when he was a child and then, as he approached the age of 50, the situation had changed little. The Reverend Lee saw what he thought to be the solution, the ballot box.

Reverend Lee had married, in 1936, a young girl, quiet and sweet and gentle, from a little community just north of Belzoni, Miss., where he was preaching. Now, nearly twenty years later, he and Rose still lived in Belzoni, the seat of Humphreys County (1954 population 7,000 whites, and 16,000 Negroes).

Lee no longer trembled at the approach of "the man" and felt that surely there must be others who did not. He ferreted out

62 of the bolder variety of Black people in 1954 and applied for a charter to the NAACP. Reverend Lee and a friend, Gus Courts, then led a voter registration drive which produced a list of 95 Black people, as well as pressure from the White Citizens Council to "forget it." Reverend Lee, however, was not of a forgetful nature nor was he afraid of death. He told his wife, who was frightened and wanted to give up, ". . . there may be some bloodshed, and it may be my blood that gets shed. If so, we'll just have to take it. At least we have no children who will suffer."

When Mrs. Lee called the hospital in Belzoni on May 7, 1955, she was told that her husband had been shot. The lower left side of his face was gone as were his jawbone and, of course, his life. One man, one vote, silenced by the blast of a shotgun.

"Rose Lee says of her martyred husband, 'He had all the signs of being somebody, if he had a chance.' Reverend George Lee died so that others, with the signs of being somebody, might have that chance.

Reverend Elijah P. Lovejoy
White man killed for supporting abolition

****Reverend Elijah P. Lovejoy**, the white editor of the St. Louis Observer, was forced to leave town for protesting the lynching of a Negro. He moved north to Alton, Illinois in 1837, where his liberal views and abolitionist ideas were met with mob resistance. When asked to leave Alton, Lovejoy replied, "Is not this a free state? . . . Have not I the right to claim protection of the laws? . . . Before God and you all, I here pledge myself to continue it, if need be till death." Reverend Lovejoy died defending his press with five bullets in his body. His death, however, "fused abolitionism and freedom of the press into a common cause."

****John Brown**, 1859, the controversial white "liberator," attacked the federal arsenal at Harper's Ferry, West Virginia, in an effort to ignite slave revolt. John Copeland, a Black participant sentenced to hang with Brown, wrote his brother from prison, "It was a sense of wrongs which we have suffered that prompted the noble but unfortunate Captain John Brown and his associates to attempt to give freedom to a small number, at least, of those who are now held by cruel and unjust men. To this freedom they were entitled by every known principle of justice and humanity. Dear brother, could I die for a more noble cause?"

On the morning of his execution, John Brown himself wrote, "I, John Brown, now am quite certain that the crimes of this guilty land will never be purged away but with blood. I had, as I now think vainly, flattered myself that without much bloodshed it might be done." . . . "On a clear, cool, sun bright morning, they rode John Brown to the scaffold in an open cart. The old man looked at the Blue Ridge Mountains in the distance and said, 'This is a beautiful country.'

THE MAN AND THE IMAGE - "Maniac or martyr?"

It has often been said that statistics can be used to prove anything one might desire to prove. In that same manner, the people and events recorded in the annals of history are often shaded by the attitudes that prevailed at that time.

A point of interest is the historical depiction of John Brown. The view that many of us hold is that John Brown was a raving, totally irresponsible maniac.

What kind of man was John Brown?

Here are a few quotes from some of the leading statesmen, writers and spokesmen of the times:

"Brown is a bundle of the best nerves I ever saw, cut and thrust, bleeding and in bonds. He is a man of clear head, of courage, fortitude. He is a fanatic, vain and garrulous, but firm and truthful and intelligent." - Virginia Governor Henry Wise

"John Brown has twice as much right to hang Governor Wise as Governor Wise has to hang him." - Boston Attorney Wendell Phillips

"In firing his gun, John Brown has merely told us what time of day it is. It is high noon, thank God!" - William Lloyd Garrison

THEY WERE FIRST...

Isaak Murphy
First jockey to win THREE Kentucky Derbies

If you can make one heap of all your winnings
    And risk it on one turn of pitch-and-toss,
And lose, and start again at your beginnings
    And never breath a word about your loss;
If you can force your heart and nerve and sinew
    To serve your turn long after they are gone,
And so hold on when there is nothing in you
    Except the Will which says to them: "Hold on!

There always have to be some who will take the chance so that others might follow; some who say "Yes I can." In every walk of life there are records to be broken, boundaries to cross, frontiers to explore. There have been people who have lost what for the moment must have seemed like everything. Notwithstanding the obstacles, men whose eyes were skyward did hold on, their wills were strong and their turns were served. Here we present a few of the many Blacks who dared challenge, who did set records, and who opened new frontiers. From those who are brave enough to challenge, mankind benefits and the world grows a little bolder.

IN THE YEAR...

1538 — **LITTLE STEPHEN ESTEVANICO**, African-born and Black, who had originally landed in the New World at Tampa Bay, Florida in 1528, led an expedition north from Mexico and discovered Arizona and New Mexico. Estevanico was one of the outstanding Spanish explorers and was instrumental in the exploration of the new world.

1731 — **BENJAMIN BANNEKER** was born and destined to become a famous astronomer, inventor, mathematician, and writer of the first American almanac. Despite his color, Mr. Banneker was appointed by George Washington as one of the planners of the city of Washington, D.C.

1762 — **DR. JAMES DERHAM** was born with, or quite possibly without, the aid of a doctor. Derham later worked out his freedom under a white doctor in New Orleans and later became recognized as America's pioneer black physician.

1790 — **JEAN BAPTISTE POINTE DUSABLE**, a French-speaking Black man, became the first permanent settler of the area at the southern end of Lake Michigan and is considered the founder of the City of Chicago. The "Windy City" took root when DuSable, a fur trader, decided to establish a trading post at the southern tip of Lake Michigan.

1810 — **TOM MOLINEAUX**, a Virginia slave, gained fame when he fought Tom Cribb in a bare-fisted boxing match in England that lasted forty rounds, becoming America's first athlete to compete abroad.

1872 — **PAUL LAURENCE DUNBAR** was born in Dayton, Ohio and went on to become the first nationally known Black poet. Dunbar published his first book at the age of twenty-one and later was invited to Queen Victoria's Diamond Jubilee to recite his poetry.

1874 — **GEORGE WILLIAMS**, who served in the Union Army at age 14, was the first Black graduate of Newton Theological Seminary in Massachusetts. Mr. Williams was also admitted as a lawyer to the Ohio Bar Association and later was noted as the foremost black historian of his generation.

1883 — **JAN MATZELIGER**, a "light-skinned" Black man, born in the 1840's in Dutch Guiana, came to the U.S. where he developed and patented a machine that revolutionized the shoe industry in 1883. Matzeliger's "lasting" machine enabled the United Shoe Manufacturing Company, which bought the invention, to control within a few years, 98 per cent of the shoe machinery trade, with a capital stock of $20,000,000 and 40 subsidiary companies.

Jan Matzeliger
Revolutionized the shoe industry

Matzeliger's invention was "capable of performing all the steps required to hold a shoe on its last, grip and pull the leather down around the heel, guide and drive the nails into place and then discharge the shoe from the machine."

1886 — **AUGUSTUS TOLTON** became, on April 24 of that year, the first Black American priest ordained in Rome. He returned to the U.S. to head a parish in Quincy, Illinois, before moving on to Chicago where he established St. Monica's Church.

1891 — **ISAAC MURPHY** won the Kentucky Derby, becoming the FIRST jockey to ever ride three winners. The Black rider had also won the classic in 1884, and 1890.

1893 — **DR. DANIEL HALE WILLIAMS** performed the world's first successful heart operation at Provident Hospital in Chicago, which he helped found in 1891. There Dr. Williams also established the first training school for Black nurses in the U.S. The papers on the day following the operation reported that Dr. Williams had "sewed up the human heart of an emergency case who had suffered a knife wound."

1894 — **DR. CHARLES R. DREW** was born and, before his death in 1950, became a renowned medical scientist in the development of blood plasma. While director of the British Blood Plasma Project, Drew introduced the revolutionary proposal for a "blood bank" resulting in today's modern "blood bank" system.

1909 — **MATHEW A. HENSON** accompanied Robert E. Peary and four Eskimos to become the first man ever to set foot on the uppermost region of the Earth, the North Pole. Henson, Peary's Black adventurer-companion, actually preceded the famous explorer by 45 minutes and was given a congressional medal and commendation from the president.

1910 — **JACK JOHNSON** won boxing's heavyweight championship of the world, another first for America's black populace.

1912 — **BENJAMIN O. DAVIS, SR.,** the first black general to serve the U.S. Army, announced the birth of Benjamin O. Davis, Jr., who was to become a general, another first, in the Air Force.

1918 — **HUGH MULZAC** received the maritime Master's License giving him the authority to operate an ocean going vessel in national and international waters. Mulzac, in 1942, was appointed the first captain of the USS Booker T. Washington.

1955 — **MARIAN ANDERSON** had come a long way from the church choir where she started in Philadelphia. In this year, Miss Anderson became the first Negro prima donna to sing with the Metropolitan Opera Company.

1961 — **LEONTYNE PRICE** became the first black singer to star in an opening night production of the Metropolitan Opera. "Cleopatra" by Samuel Barber was later composed especially for her. She ultimately received the Order of Merit of the Italian Republic.

1965 — **CONSTANCE BAKER MOTLEY** became the president of the Borough of Manhattan in New York City and was the highest paid Negro woman in municipal government. She subsequently became the first black woman to serve as a federal judge.

1965 — **MRS. PATRICIA R. HARRIS** was assigned to Luxembourg as an Ambassador, the first woman of her race to be so honored. Mrs. Harris, who graduated first in her class at George Washington University Law School, was chosen by President Johnson to fill the position.

1966 — **ROBERT C. WEAVER** was announced as the first Negro ever to be appointed to a presidential Cabinet. Mr. Weaver, an economist and administrator of the Federal Housing and Home Finance Agency, had previously served as a housing authority in President Roosevelt's "Black Cabinet" in 1938.

OTHERS "ORGANIZED"…

Richard Allen
Founder: African Methodist Episcopal Church

If you can talk with crowds and keep your virtue,
 Or walk with kings--nor lose the common touch,
If neither foes nor loving friends can hurt you;
 If all men count with you, but none too much,
If you can fill the unforgiving minute
 With sixty seconds' worth of distance run,
Yours is the Earth and everything that's in it,
 And--which is more--you'll be a Man, my son!

—Rudyard Kipling

At the end of one's life, they invariably gaze backwards for a retrospective summation of their achievements. Fortunate is the person whose life is such that it helps produce viable institutions in order to benefit others. Generally, these are the people who are able to organize not only their thoughts, but also the people they influence. The apostle of a new movement is always in the vanguard of society. History will reveal the products of their toil and praise... or ignore their legacy.

Those black leaders who chose to emblazon in the annuls of time the principles and ideas for which they stood, will live as long as do the institutions that pass on the fruits of their labors.

RICHARD ALLEN (1760-1831) was pulled from his knees one Sunday while at prayer by a white usher in the St. George Methodist Episcopal Church in Philadelphia. A resolute and determined Mr. Allen then started his own movement and in 1794 founded the African Methodist Episcopal Church in Philadelphia so that he and his people might pray in peace and dignity.

THOMAS PAUL established in 1809 the African Baptist Church in Boston and a few years later helped organize the Abyssinian Baptist Church in New York. Today it is the largest church of Baptist denomination in the world and is located in Harlem.

LOTT CARY bought his own freedom as well as that of his family before organizing the Richmond African Baptist Missionary Society in 1850. He then took leave of America and journeyed to Africa in order to personally spread his work, becoming one of the earliest missionaries to the "Dark Continent."

ROBERT S. ABBOTT was born in 1870 and at the age of 35 founded the Chicago Defender with himself as editor. Mr. Abbott weathered many a storm in his efforts to keep the Black people of Chicago informed. His paper was the most influential and militant of all Black newspapers at the dawn of the 20th century.

CARTER G. WOODSON (1875-1950) made possible the teaching of Black history in colored schools and colleges. He did so through his Association for the Study of Negro Life and History established in 1915, three years after he received his doctorate from Harvard.

Harriet Tubman
Incredible story

Every so often there emerges from the masses a person who has determination and stamina beyond all comprehension. When Harriet Tubman died in 1913, around the age of 90, she left a record of incredible indomitability.

What sort of longing caused young Harriet, when in her mid-twenties, to leave her parents, brothers and sisters on a plantation in Maryland to follow the "North Star" to freedom? Further yet, why did she RETURN, not only to rescue her parents, but more than three hundred others? All told, she made 19 trips under the cover of darkness into the perilous, southern states. So important a "conductor" in the "underground railroad" was Harriet, that a $40,000 reward was offered for her capture.

A few years after her own escape, President Millard Fillmore signed, in 1850, the New Fugitive Slave Law. For this reason Harriet found it necessary to take her passengers all the way to Canada so the slaves wouldn't be returned by scavengers. Once in Canada, Harriet turned to the arduous task of caring for her adopted brood through their first northern winter.

In the spring she would return for more passengers. Harriet, by this time, had made contacts with a number of whites and free Blacks who assisted her with food, clothing and shelter, risking their lives to do so. "Way Stations" or check points were about twenty miles apart stretching from the Mason Dixon Line all the way to the Canadian border. Harriet ventured southward to lead her people, frightened and trembling, to freedom.

Once there beneath the North Star, each escaped slave must have felt as Harriet did when she said, "I looked at my hands to see if I was de same person now I was free. Dere was such a glory ober everything! De sun come like gold thru de trees and ober de fields, and I felt like I was in Heaven."

When the Civil War erupted in 1861 the Confederates were surprised to find themselves harassed by what must have seemed like the ghost of the little Black lady from Maryland.

Amazing though it seemed, Harriet, nearing 40 years of age, had joined the Union Army as a nurse, scout and intelligence agent. General Saxton reported "she made many a raid inside the enemy lines, displaying remarkable courage, zeal and fidelity."

One might wonder why this magnificent lady is included in this section. What exactly did Harriet "found" or organize? She founded a deep personal sense of freedom that compelled her to share it; she found the courage to risk that same freedom in order to share it; she found the fears and despair of a "whole bunch" of Black folks and gave them hope and a dream in return. As Harriet Tubman once said of her underground train to freedom, "I nebber run my train off de track and I nebber lost a passenger."

PROGRESS...

Yes, it is VERY important to acknowledge that progress toward equality for ALL people has been and is being made - here in the USA and around the world; yet we have so very far to go. It IS important to note that **Colin Powell** became the first Black U.S. Secretary of State (2001);

...that **Condoleezza Rice** was the first Black WOMAN in that position (2005);

…that **Oprah Winfrey**, born to an unwed teenage mother in Mississippi in 1954, became the richest African-American of the 20th century and the greatest Black philanthropist in American history;

…also, that Black rapper **"Iced Tea"** was vilified early in his career for recordings that "glamorized killing police officers," admitted to a "life of crime" in this early years… but <u>currently</u> (again 2012) portrays a detective on the NBC-TV police drama "Law & Order: Special Victims Unit" … CATCHIN' the bad guys!!!! Progress.

And, yes, **Barack Obama**, a Black man, was elected President of the United States of America in 2008!

Now... that LAST section just may be the most important part of this publication. **Progress** toward a more just, open, peaceful, cooperative, and healthy society is, logically, in the best interest of us ALL. Please... go back to the question at the beginning of this "little booklet," and ask yourself... "how much better could life be for all of us, if we had just done the right thing(s) in the first place? Remember the past! But forget the anger... let's be honest with ourselves and get on with the future! If not for our own sakes, for our children, grandchildren, and future generations.

In the name of Peace, Progress, Good Health, Mutual Respect, and Increasing Prosperity for all,

Walter G. (Buzz) Luttrell

EPILOGUE...

This little "booklet" is intended to be interesting without sensationalism and informative without factual deluge. I have tried to illustrate a few simple points, using highlights of the often ignored Black side of American history.

First, Black Americans have made many contributions to this country and the world, under the most extreme circumstances and obstacles.

Secondly, the freedom and privileges accorded white Americans have long been denied to Blacks, for whom opportunity has come at a premium in the "Land of Opportunity."

Third, this country has reached an impasse which demands unity while also affording freedom of individual expression. There must be respect and conformity in regard to the laws that govern us, and there will be, if those laws are blind to color and human condition.

Few respect a person who will not defend their honor and dignity as a human being: the description most often used is "coward." Thus, it should not be shocking when we find Black Americans demanding their rights as first class citizens.

Finally, in reference to that perpetual question, "what do 'they' want?" We suggest that others, in turn, ask of themselves, "what would I want if I were Black (or any other color for that matter)".

James Baldwin once wrote, "It is only when, without bitterness or self-pity, a man (person) is able to surrender a dream (they) have long cherished or a privilege (they) have long possessed that (they) are free; (they) have set (themselves) free for higher dreams, for greater privileges." *(author changes in parentheses)*

Once we reject the notion that the color of one's skin, or nationality, religion, or creed makes that person inherently superior or inferior, we can get on with the greatest challenge facing this rapidly evolving "global community" - building a better world for all people.

Author
WHAT THE WORLD SHOULD KNOW ABOUT...
BLACK HISTORY IN THE USA

Walter (Buzz) Luttrell first wrote the core of this publication in 1969 as an educational supplement (Black America's Echoes of The Past) for distribution to public schools by a public relations client. Recently, he was very disappointed to hear from a variety of young students that, aside from "Black History Month," there is still very little light shed on "the Black experience" in the U.S. in their history courses. For that reason, he updated and modified the "booklet" as a stimulating, easy-to-read, but "challenging primer" for those interested in further exploring or teaching about Black history in the USA.

Luttrell was born (1944) and raised in small-town Allegan, Michigan. He graduated from Olivet College (MI) and worked in banking, public relations, television, and corporate communications. At WXYZ-TV Detroit he was community affairs director, talk show host, and an award-winning reporter. At WBZ-TV Boston he was a two-time Emmy-winning talk-show host. Always determined to convince his employers to support "public service" projects, Luttrell initiated the "image campaign" that helped Detroit shake the label "Murder Capital of the World" and gain media coverage as "The Renaissance City in the mid-70's;" created a television campaign, "The Best of the Class," that eventually saluted **inner-city** high school valedictorians in over 90 U.S. cities; and received the U.S. Justice Department's "Community Service Award" for the nationally-distributed educational video, "The Possible Dream - Racial Harmony in U.S. Schools." He lives today outside Boston, MA and is working to promote the concept of "global community" and the importance of understanding the *interdependence* of ALL countries on a healthy "global economy."

RESEARCH CREDITS

Hughes, Langston and Meltzer, Milton, A Pictorial History of the Negro in America, New York: Crown Publishers, Inc., 1956

Lot, Philip Henry, Ph.D., Rising Above Color, New York: Fleming H. Revell Company, 1943

Mendelson, Jack, The Martyrs, New York: Harper & Row, 1966

Slak, Erwin A., A Layman's Guide to Negro History, Chicago: Quadrangle Books, 1966

PHOTO/IMAGE CREDITS

"The Thinker," by Rodin, photog. Andrew Horne, Public Domain

John Chavis, Public Domain, source Helen Chavis Othow

George Washington Carver, Public Domain, Source: Linda O. McMurry, *George Washington Carver: Scientist and Symbol* (New York: Oxford University Press, 1981)

Crispus Attucks, published in US before 1923, Public Domain

Reverend Elijah P. Lovejoy, Public Domain, Source= "Appletons' Cyclopaedia of American Biography," 1900

John Brown, by Augustus Washington, 1846-47, © expired

Isaak Murphy, Public Domain, date on photo 1885. Author J.H. Fenton

Jan Matzeliger, 1885, author unknown, © expired, Public Domain

Marian Anderson, Public Domain, Library of Congress, Reproduction number LC-USZ62-42524, Author, Carl Van Vechten (1880-1964)

Richard Allen, by Daniel A Payne, 1891, © expired, Public Domain

Harriet Tubman, picture from the Famous People: Selected Portraits From the Collection of the Library of Congress, date unknown, Public Domain, Unique image ID: 7147df7e5ec6b854d6e10137c818437a

Colin Powell, Public Domain/US Gov.

Oprah Winfrey, Public Domain, source BlackPast.org, Catherine D. (Kay) Foster

President Barack Obama, Public Domain, U.S. Gov.

SPECIAL THANKS: Scott Anderson, for helping edit, revise, and publish this booklet. Without his personal help, moral support, incredible breadth of knowledge of all things intellectual and technical, this publication might never have been made available to the world as an eBook and as a thought-provoking "hardcopy booklet" for schools, libraries... and your coffee table.

www.ingramcontent.com/pod-product-compliance
Lightning Source LLC
Chambersburg PA
CBHW080832310526
45788CB00019B/3257